Also by the author:

Weird Shit Happened And There Were Crystals.
A Spiritual memoir (of sorts)

Coming soon:

The Hollywood Diaries

A Waiter Wrote Some Haikus

By

Dave Sanderson

Copyright ©2022 Dave Sanderson. All Rights Reserved

For Dylan and Bodhi with love always.

To the girls in the flower shop, thank you for being great neighbours.

A Waiter Wrote Some Haikus

By

Dave Sanderson

Introduction

Hello dear reader and Thank you buying my first book of Haikus.

I just want you to know that technically I've lied to you. Yeah, I'm sorry, I know this isn't a great start to our Author/reader relationship.

I am the victim of my own lack of knowledge, let me tell you a story....
You see, this fun little project began while working on my hopefully forthcoming Hollywood Diaries book.

I was struck down with undiagnosed man-flu/common cold and I can assure you that I found myself feeling quite close to death.

I struggled on regardless, like the brave little soldier I am, and though I didn't have the energy to continue with the Hollywood book, I needed to do something creative, just to get it out of my system. I wrote what I thought were 20 or so Haiku's that day between lengthy naps.

Every time something popped into my head, or was inspired by the TV or radio, I made it into a Haiku.
A few weeks later when I had recovered I had 50 written.

I realised that the collection of 3 lined, 17 syllable poems, captured current events and pop culture as well as giving an insight on being a waiter, my life and to some degree, my weird fragile little mind.

With a little research, I discovered that Haikus focus on nature, while what I have created are more akin to Senryu, (pronounced Senroo)
a poem with the same structure as Haiku, but focusing on the self and life with a cynical/satirical twist.

Yeah, that sounds like me.

With enough written I figured I'd put them in a book, and so here we are me and you, you and me, counting syllables on our fingers together.

Enjoy.

The honest title....

A Waiter Wrote Some Senryus

(But more people have heard of Haikus)

By

Dave Sanderson

A Waiter wrote some Senryus about.....

.....Writing and Haikus

First line must be five

The second line is seven

Then five to finish

I'd do this all day

But it doesn't pay the rent

Or my other bills

A book of Haikus

Am I out of my damn mind?

Na, you bought this shit.

Yeah sex is great, but

Have you ever written a

Book of haikus?

I feel rough as fuck

So I've been writing haikus

To amuse myself

I wrote a poem

And then I wrote 15 more

A new book started

A creative spark

Is controlled by syllables

On this very page

Bullshit in my head

Spilled onto a white page

For others to read

I would write much more

If I just put my phone down.

Procrastination!

Can I make it work?

The Hollywood Diaries book

I guess we'll soon know.

Five, a slice of bread

Seven, the tasty filling

Five, another bread slice

While others find sleep

The night is quiet and calm

I write endlessly

The pen and a page

Have become a counsellor

To share my thoughts with

Counting syllables

On my fingers for each line

Poetic numbers

A Waiter wrote some Senryus about.....

...Waitering

Bring us lots of drinks

The food is secondary

At bottomless brunch

Any Allergies?

Card payments only ok?

Follow me this way.

Make yourself comfy

I'll come back for a drink order

In a few minutes

You're not ready yet

Please don't make me watch you read

I've got things to do

Pina Colada?

Bit basic, but yeah go off

I'll go ring it in.

Starter and main course

Extra cheese on everything

Drinks a diet coke

You ignored the sign:

'Please wait here to be seated'

Slow service for you

Oh, you're SO lovely

You are now a crush-tomer

My daydreamer love

Here to make your day

Bring your food and drinks quickly

All done with a smile

A shift that's so bad

Suicidal tendencies

On the drive back home

Forty five years old

Still a damned waiter

I've made bad choices

You can't be vegan

Because you haven't told me

You're vegan four times

Did you seat yourself

At this one dirty table

Only to complain?

Where is the rota?

How is it still not done yet?

Every week we wait.

I'm in no mood

For post work drinks at the pub

Too many people

A chaotic shift

Shit the moment I arrive

I need a new job

The mind is willing

Sometimes my body says no

If I work too hard

Forty five year old

Waiter. But I've had enough now

Can we lock the doors?

A Waiter Wrote some Senryus about....

...The seasons

        Leaves crunch under foot

        Breath visible in the air

        I long for summer

Laying on the beach

Soaking up the suns warm rays

Reading a good book

Little hints of green

Nature starting to wake up

Summer is coming

A Waiter Wrote Some Senryus about...

...life's little moments

Binge watching Netflix

A human shaped sofa dent

Are you still watching?

You're going too slow

Stupid middle lane hogger

On the motorway

My whole body hurts

Will this be the end of me

Or is it man-flu?

Who's got the remote?

Are you sat on it again?

Stand up and show me

Dentist waiting room

The nervous silence broken

By a drilling sound

Cute pink nurses scrubs

Gorgeous dental hygienist

Face mask pretty eyes.

A lottery win

Two pounds fifty a ticket,

Perpetual hope

BMW owner

I can tell you're a cunt

By the way you drive

Despite the chaos

Our eyes held each other's gaze

A connection made

Page sixty

This is page sixty

Are we being entertained?

Have I done my job?

No-one teaches us

How to deal with our own grief

Until we've known death

A Waiter Wrote Some Senryus inspired by....

...Film and TV

This is our town now

We're in charge. By order of

The Peaky Blinders

First and second rule

We don't talk about fight club

Do you understand?

Han and Chewie on

The Millennium Falcon

Scruffy Nerf herders

Kirk to Enterprise

I'm busy shagging green girls

Do not beam me up

Trash can shaped robot

Brave little R2 unit

Beep boop beep beep boop

Captain Jack Sparrow

Why is the rum always gone?

You great big lummox

Vengeance roams the night

Bringing evil to justice

He is the Batman

Vodka martini

Womaniser with a gun

The name's Bond. James Bond.

But you've still not seen

The Princess Bride? I find this

Inconceivable!

Beautiful weathergirl

Stunning eyes and smile

You are the sunshine

To build my own place

And to appear on Grand Designs

With Kevin McCloud

A Waiter Wrote some Senryus about...

..Himself
(which get a little dark)

Feel disconnected

Taking care of customers

Then back home alone.

I've wanted to die

I've seen no point to my life

I know that dark place

End my suffering

But pass it on to others?

No choice but to live

Fought, kicked, screamed, cried, hurt.

And got so much counselling

To save my own life

I healed and took time

To get myself right again

Nearly there, maybe.

Please buy all my books

I'm over Waitering now

Too old for that shit

A song, a person

A musical connection

A soundtrack. My life.

Page seventy nine

Page seventy nine

Thank you for reading this far

I'll wrap this up soon

Hero or villain

I can be both. Depending

On your narrative

Post-funeral sex

Need to feel alive after

Being close to death.

Billionaire me

Would be a philanthropist

For a better world

Reading through this book

A few ups and a few downs

Much like my own life

Though I may not think

I'm resilient as fuck

I've been through some shiiiiit

For the love of God

Let me win the lottery

Please, please, please, please, please.

I dream of my own

VW campervan

A split screen classic

My anger tells me

When I'm being treated wrong

Valid emotion

A daddy of two

Bohemian, a loner

Blue eyes, pirate smile

I try to ignore

The negative voice I hear

In my busy mind

Witty old fucker

Sitting alone with humour

Amusing himself

Not enough money

For midlife crisis sports car

So I write poems

My walls are up

Keep people at a distance

So I can't get hurt

I have lived and died

More times than I can recall

Old soul, achy foot.

A Waiter Wrote some Senryus about.....

...His Kids

Dylan and Bodhi

My two greatest creations

I love you SO much

Its parents evening

Teacher says all the right things

My kids, good people.

Thoughtful, kind, polite

Full of effort, funny, smart

And inquisitive

A Waiter wrote some Senryus about.....

...The Flat above the flower shop

A writer who lives

Above a flower shop is

Main character vibes

He returns to the

Flat above the flower shop

Happy to be home

Two giggling girlies

In the flower shop below

Best neighbours ever

A summer morning

Windows down sound system up

Turning heads outside

Kitchen window vibes

Looking down Union Street

As rain starts to fall

Metal guttering

Plays music under rainfall

Tiny plinky plinks

A Waiter wrote some Senryus about.....

...Politics

I hate the Tories

What they've done to the country

It's criminal, right?

The cost of living

Should be service to others

Not a full time job

We hold our waiters

To higher standards than our

Shitty government

Some things in my fridge

Lasted longer than Liz Truss

And they're still in date

Dead for showing hair

Iranian women unite

Fight for your freedoms

Dystopian shit

Twelve year old opens food bank

For hungry neighbours

The enemy doth arrive

By private jet, dear reader

Not by rubber boat

Your kids are safer

With a drag queen, than with a

Member of clergy

A Waiter Wrote some Senryus about...

...Her
(then he considered more counselling)

                I'll always love you

        But you couldn't treat me right

              Your loss gas lighter

Red haired green eyed girl

The one that almost broke me

I'm stronger than you

Thought we were for keeps

I thought we'd be forever

You sold me a lie

I'll wait. At some point

Your lies will catch up with you

They'll see you darlin'.

Creepy and weird huh?

And yet you called me soul mate

Which lie is the truth?

I carry trauma

Because of how you played me

Now you play others

What you did to me

Not forgiven or forgot

Karma waits for you

I saw you today

Bloated, pale, tired looking

You've lost your shine babe

A Waiter Wrote a Haiku...

Icy white tundra

Snow in every direction

An arctic fox hunts

A Waiter Wrote some Senryus about ..

...Random subjects

Teardrops down windows

Is it raining outside now?

Or am I crying

Chocolate digestives

You are so very more-ish

Just one more perhaps

Goddess like body

Pressed hard against mine. We move

And find ecstasy.

Throw away the map

Let's go on an adventure

A road less travelled

The ingredients

Roach, paper, tobacco and weed

Roll, smoke, and chill out

Brave little red fox

Makes his way past us, limping

As he looks for food

Are these any good

Or am I delusional

A bit of both huh?

And yet you're still here

Like a turd that won't flush

Stinking up the place

I daydream too much

Of things that will never be

Things like you and me

Finish on a high

Something uplifting and bright

Can I find the words?

A Waiter Wrote a Haiku to send you on your way...

Go now, be at peace

Carry love with you always

Be kind to others

Coming soon

The Hollywood Diaries

By

Dave Sanderson

Printed in Great Britain
by Amazon